Camping

Food On Stick Recipes

Louise Davidson

All rights reserved © 2022 by Louise Davidson and The Cookbook Publisher. No part of this publication or the information in it may be quoted from or reproduced in any form by means such as printing, scanning, photocopying, or otherwise without prior written permission of the copyright holder.

This book is presented solely for motivational and informational purposes. The author and the publisher do not hold any responsibility for errors, omissions, or contrary interpretation of the subject matter herein.

The recipes provided in this book are for informational purposes only and are not intended to provide dietary advice. A medical practitioner should be consulted before making any changes in diet. Additionally, recipes' cooking times may require adjustment depending on age and quality of appliances. Readers are strongly urged to take all precautions to ensure ingredients are fully cooked to avoid the dangers of foodborne illnesses. The recipes and suggestions provided in this book are solely the opinions of the author. The author and publisher do not take any responsibility for any consequences that may result due to following the instructions provided in this book.

All the nutritional information contained in this book is provided for informational purposes only. This information is based on the specific brands, ingredients, and measurements used to make the recipe, and therefore the nutritional information is an estimate, and in no way is intended to be a guarantee of the actual nutritional value of the recipe made in the reader's home. The author and the publisher will not be responsible for any damages resulting in your reliance on the nutritional information. The best method to obtain an accurate count of the nutritional value in the recipe is to calculate the information with your specific brands, ingredients, and measurements.

ISBN 9798811222964

Printed in the United States

— THE —
COOK BOOK
PUBLISHER

www.thecookbookpublisher.com

CONTENTS

INTRODUCTION 1

SAFETY AROUND THE FIRE AND COOKING IN THE GREAT OUTDOORS 5

BREAKFAST 13

APPETIZERS AND SIDES 21

CHICKEN 31

BEEF, PORK, AND LAMB 43

SEAFOOD 57

VEGETARIAN 63

DESSERTS 71

RECIPE INDEX 81

APPENDIX 83

INTRODUCTION

Whether you are new to this form of cooking, simply interested, or already habitually stoking fire frequently for the pleasure of family and friends, this cookbook was specifically made for you.

Camping Cookbook Food on Stick Recipes will take you on a tour of cooking on a stick when camping in all its contemporary forms. It includes lots of flavor-packed recipes, tips, and safety measures.

Campfire cooking on a stick encompasses a wide range of techniques, from barbequing, grilling, and baking to roasting and smoking, and the foundation of a wide variety of cuisines from worldwide.

While camping, you are less likely to have all the things you want for cooking, but you don't need one to use this book. I believe while cooking on a campfire, your recipes have to be as simple as possible. So, all of the recipes in this cookbook are drawn to bring campfire cooking on a stick to an easy, enjoyable, and simple form.

This cookbook covers all of the most common cooking on a stick techniques when camping, including grilling, baking, barbeque, and cooking over a campfire. This book will show you how to cook on a stick without any specific appliance.

Back to the dawn of fire cooking dates, you will learn how to prepare deliciously flavorful food for your family and friends. So, let's get started on our scorching adventure.

Measuring Temperature in Campfire Cooking

Since you're going to find yourself cooking outdoors without your usual kitchen equipment, it may be a challenge to know exactly the campfire's cooking temperature. But worry not as there's a simple way for you to get a rough estimate of a fire's temperature when campfire cooking and it's called the "hand test."

To do this test, all you have to do is hover your hand just above the cooking area (about 12 inches). The duration you're able to hold out your hand over the heat will give you an estimate of the fire's temperature.

<1 second: 600°F or 316°C (high)
1-2 seconds: 400-500°F or 204-260°C (medium-high)
3-4 seconds: 350-375°F or 177-191°C (medium)
5-7 seconds: 325-350°F or 163-177°C (low)

That's it. **Please be careful not to burn your hand when doing this test**.

Tips and Safety Measures for Cooking on a Stick When Camping

- Your wood should be dead and not green, preferably dry, so your fire will be constructed in a manner that allows decent airflow to it.
- Use 2 logs on the bottom to construct 2 sides, 2 logs on the top overlapping the edges of these and at right angles to form the other 2 sides, and so on.
- Never use petrol to burn the fire; always use matches, a gas torch, taper, or a ball of paper on the end of the stick to light the campfire.
- Always wait until the larger piece of wood has collapsed the fire.
- Always take foil with you when you are going camping as it helps in cooking.
- Test the stability of the heavy food on the campfire. Rectify any fault before lighting the coal.
- Always take a set of metal tongs with rubber/plastic handles.
- Take metal or bamboo skewers along with you while camping.
- Always soak the bamboo skewers for at least 30 minutes before cooking.
- Try to burn your campfire where people will not constantly be walking past it.
- Do not place your campfire under the hanging trees.
- Keep away the things from the campfire that could easily burn as sparks from campfires while cooking could ignite nearby paper, wood, fabric, plastic, etc.
- Move any fuel sources, lighters, petrol cans, tins, and paint away from the cooking area.
- Always put a bucket of water near the campfire, just in case.
- Make sure there is always someone looking after the fire while cooking.
- Fat from meat can cause tiny fires, so someone should always be there to douse them as they begin.

- Never let children go near the campfire.
- After cooking, cover the coal with sand or douse it well with water.

Tips on Making Campfire Biscuit Cups

One of the best recipes you can make with a stick is making campfire biscuit cups that you then fill with favorite ingredients, be it sweet or savory. You find several campfire biscuit cups recipes in this cookbook. And the best is that campers can personalize them to their liking. Here are a few tips to make the perfect biscuit cups.

- You can use either biscuit dough or crescent roll dough. Though the crescent roll dough may require more forming and fussing.
- For the dough sizes, it's best to use Junior sizes. A technique you can try that may result in the least tearing of holes in the dough is to take the round piece of the dough and put it on a semi-non-stick surface. Using your fingers, pat the dough into a flat circle, about 3 inches in diameter. Hold it and drop the dough onto the stick. Press and form around the cup.
- Wood or metal are both okay to use, oiled or not. Though on metal, the added oil may prevent the dough from holding its shape when being baked. A spritz of cooking spray also worked well on dowel form models.
- If the outside is done but the inside is raw after cooking, you can carefully remove the baked cup from the form and place the cup, open side down, above a fire grate for a few minutes until it is cooked.
- Special sticks are now available on the market that makes it easy to make biscuit cups. Brands that are popular include Woof'Em sticks or Mini Cobbler sticks. They are available online. The dough can be stretched on the sticks to for a nice biscuit cups ready to be filled with savory or sweet ingredients you choose.

SAFETY AROUND THE FIRE AND COOKING IN THE GREAT OUTDOORS

In the next section, we discuss food safety at the campsite, what to bring on your camping trip, and general cooking tips. To go directly to the recipes, go to page 13.

Food Safety Reminders

I would not feel comfortable without any words on food safety and this is especially true when you are on the road or at the campsite.

When cooking outdoors, it is important to be diligent when it comes to food safety. Whether you have a portable refrigerator in your camper or you are depending upon your trusty cooler and ice or ice packs, keeping perishable foods at a temperature of 40°F or lower is priority number one. It takes barely any time at all for food-borne bacteria to invade your perishables.

It is a good idea to bring along, at least one, if not several food thermometers to monitor the temperature of foods both during refrigeration and during cooking. Also, never leave cooked food sitting out too long. Once you are finished eating, any leftovers should be properly packaged and refrigerated. Always thoroughly wash any working surface where raw ingredients have been resting or worked on including cutting boards and tools.

When handling, cooking, and storing food, safe steps need to be taken and shouldn't be taken likely. It's important to observe food safety measures as it helps prevent the spread of foodborne illnesses. Harmful bacteria cannot be detected through sight, smell, or taste.

That's why with every step of food preparation, these four rules must be followed:

- **Clean**—Disinfect hands and surfaces often.
- **Separate**—Do not store raw meat with other foods.
- **Cook**—Cook to the right temperature.
- **Chill**—Do not delay food refrigeration.

Make sure that you cook your food to these minimum internal temperatures as measured with a food thermometer before removing food from the heat source. If desired, consumers may choose to cook food at higher temperatures.

Product	Minimum Internal Temperature and Rest Time
Beef, Pork, Veal & Lamb Steaks, chops, roasts	145°F (62.8 °C) and allow to rest for at least 3 minutes
Ground Meats	160°F (71.1 °C)
Ground Poultry	165°F (73.9 °C)
Ham, fresh or smoked (uncooked)	145°F (62.8 °C) and allow to rest for at least 3 minutes
Fully-Cooked Ham (to be reheated)	Reheat cooked hams packaged in USDA-inspected plants to 140°F (60°C) and all others to 165°F (73.9°C).
All Poultry (breast, whole, leg, thigh, wing, ground, giblet, and stuffing)	165°F (73.9°C)
Eggs	160°F (71.1°C)
Fish and Shellfish	145°F (62.8°C)
Leftovers	165°F (73.9°C)
Casseroles	165°F (73.9°C)

Source: Food Safety and Inspection Service, USDA

Much of the cooking within this book refers to the open-flame style of cooking. Fire safety is essential. Always keep an eye on the fire, never leave it unattended, and make sure

that the fire is completely out, even if it is in a fire ring. Keep fire extinguishers at the ready, just in case.

Second, fire cooking is a tricky business. Until you know how to judge the heat of a fire or its coals, you may have some challenges first. The best way to attain success is to keep vigilant while cooking. Note that the best way to cook is directly on hot coals. This means you must have the time to start a fire, make it hot, and then let it die down into coals.

If you do not have this time or patience, you might want to consider alternatives, as cooking over a flame though good, is trickier. Using a grill is helpful, and moving the food consistently may help prevent scorching. If you do not feel comfortable cooking over an open flame, any camp stove will work quite well.

Do not forget to put the fire out after you are finished using it. One of the best ways to do this is to cover it with sand or dirt until it dies off completely.

Here are some additional tips regarding food safety. While this list is by no means exhaustive, it is a good starting point.

- Washing your hands before and after handling food is an important safety rule to follow at all times. It may be even more so when cooking outside. You can also use hand sanitizers.
- Working on a clean surface, and keeping bugs and undesired creepy crawlers out of your food supply is also vital to avoid food poisoning. If you can, keeping your cooler in your car or trailer is a really good way to avoid contamination.
- Wash your fruits and vegetables with safe, drinkable water.
- Drink from bottles you've bought or brought from home to make sure the water supply you use is safe to drink.
- Clean up immediately after each meal, storing leftover food in airtight containers and away from night prowlers.

Food Security
All that said, special care should be taken when preparing your foods on site. Many of these recipes include foods that require refrigeration. Keep all foods in a cooler filled with ice or in a

refrigerator until cooking. This is especially true for raw meats, dairy, and eggs. When preparing raw meats (and eggs), be careful not to cross-contaminate. This is when raw meat juices spread to other foods, like vegetables, which may be left raw.

This is a problem because botulism and other bacteria can cause serious illness when consumed, even in small quantities. Make sure to wash hands, knives, and prep materials between each dish. Keeping a cutting board and knives for each food item (green for vegetables, white for meat, for example) can help prevent cross-contamination. You may wish to prepare as much as possible before your camping trip.

Some Essentials
To Bring on Your Trip

For the fire
Waterproof matches or a few good lighters
Starter liquid fluid
Starter wood
Charcoals (plenty of it)
Cooking utensils for barbecue tongs, spatula, extra-long forks, cleaning brush for the grill.
Grill (for over the fire, if the campsite does not provide or you like having your own)
A grate to place directly on the fire to cook food on the open flame

To prepare and cook the food
Pie irons, cast iron is preferable for even cooking and durability.
Large cast-iron skillet or metal skillet that can be placed on the grill or fire
Saucepan
Heavy-duty aluminum foil
A cooking spray of your choice.
Olive oil, butter
Salt and pepper and other seasonings you may want to use, like garlic powder, chili powder, and other spices.
Oven mitts (preferably silicone to accommodate very high temperatures)
Can opener
Bottle opener
Prepping knives, cutting board
Whisk, spoons, wooden spoon, slotted spoon
Grater, vegetable peeler
Plastic strainer
Large unbreakable serving plates
Mixing bowl, various size
Measuring cups and spoons
Wood skewers
Ziplock bags
Mason jars – great for mixing dressings and has many other uses

To keep the food
One cooler with plenty of ice or ice packs to keep perishable food and drinks fresh
A second cooler or large plastic covered bin for a dry non-perishable item like cans, pasta, rice, cereals, seasoning and spices.
Plastic wrap
Plastic airtight containers for food leftover storage

To eat
Non-breakable plates, glass, cups, mugs, utensils
Napkins
Plastic tablecloth
Water bottles

To clean-up
Paper towels
Washing clothes, drying clothes
Dishwashing tub, dishwashing soap

Prep Early to Make Camping More Fun

You can make cooking at the campsite even easier on yourself by doing some of the food prep at home. Plastic food storage bags with secure closures are great for carrying premade ingredients in. They can be washable or disposable depending on your preference, they can easily be labeled, and they are the most compact way of storing food in small spaces.

When preparing food at home for the campsite, you have a couple of different options. With some dishes, you can prepare all of the ingredients and combine them together in one container so that all you need to do is transfer them from the container they will be cooked in. If you find that many of the dishes that you plan on preparing to use the same ingredients, you can prepare larger quantities of those ingredients and store them in a plastic bag, retrieving only what you need at any given time. You can also prepare each set of ingredients for dishes separately, bag and label it, and then assemble it at the campsite.

When camping, you don't have to give up homemade flavor in favor of convenience foods. However certain premade, canned, and frozen foods not only save you time but can also be easily enhanced with just a few small additions. For example, a jarred sauce with the addition of a few spices will taste heavenly and save you the extra time and ingredients of creating it from scratch.

Always pack a little extra. You never know when you will want seconds or meet a new mouth to feed. Welcome others into your campsite and make new friends and memories around your cast iron Dutch oven.

A Few Campsite Cooking Hacks

Listed below are some campsite cooking hacks that are not only innovative but very effective.

- Store dry herbs and spices in old Tic Tac® boxes.
- Aluminum foil is the best way to pack food because you can cook it over the fire during camping. Do remember to bring lots with you! If you plan to cook in foil, make sure to get the heavy-duty foil, it's more resistant to heat and you will use less.
- If possible, bring along a Dutch oven. Using this, you can try countless delicious recipes for everything from pizza and cakes to soups and stews.
- You can make an omelet by boiling it in a Ziploc® bag until the eggs are set.
- Precooking bacon or sausages at home saves a lot of time and mess at the campsite.
- Before leaving home, clean empty condiment bottles and fill them with pancake batter, cake batter, or premixed omelets to take along with you for an easy meal.
- When you open the packets, be careful of the hot steam escaping. Do not allow small children to open hot packets.

Ready to make some delicious food on a stick? Let's gets started!

BREAKFAST

Cree Bannock Bread

Bannock is a variety of quick bread baked or cooked from grains.

Serves 6 | Prep. time 30 minutes | Cooking time 30 minutes

Ingredients
3 cups flour
½ cups butter
1½ teaspoons salt
1½ teaspoons baking powder
1 cup raisins, optional
1¾ cups low-fat milk or water
Fruits and honey for serving (optional)

Skewers, either metal or bamboo

Directions
1. If using bamboo skewers, let them soak 30 minutes in water before using.
2. In a medium bowl, add the flour and butter; mix with hands.
3. Add the salt, baking powder, and raisins.
4. Add the milk and mix to make a dough.
5. Divide the dough into egg-sized lumps and wrap each lump around the end of the sticks.
6. Cook them around the fire until golden brown.
7. Serve with fruits and honey.

Nutrition per serving
Calories 208, fat 9 mg, carbs 30 g,
Protein 6 g, sodium 546 mg

Stick Bread

Bread is famous for use in breakfasts. This breadstick is easy to make by mixing flour, sugar, yeast, oil, salt, and water without kneading.

Serves 4 | Prep. time 10 minutes | Cooking time 10 minutes

Ingredients
½ teaspoon dry yeast
½ teaspoon sugar
1¼ cups flour
¼ cup + 2 tablespoons warm water
1 tablespoon olive oil
½ teaspoon salt
Sauce or dip for serving (optional)

4 metal or bamboo skewers

Directions
1. If using bamboo skewers, let them soak 30 minutes in water before using.
2. In a medium-large bowl, add all the ingredients and mix into a moist dough; no need to knead.
3. Cover the dough with a lid and let it rest for 1 hour in a warm place.
4. Put the dough onto a clean, floured surface and divide it into 4 equal pieces.
5. Start stretching the dough into the strip, and then roll it into a sausage shape.
6. Twist the dough around the end of the skewers.
7. Pinch the dough ends to secure them on the skewers.
8. Cook the bread over the campfire for 10 minutes while rotating the skewers for even cooking; serve with peanut butter and Nutella.

Nutrition per serving
Calories 148, fat 4 g, carbs 25 g, sugar 1 g,
Protein 3 g, sodium 292 mg

Croissant Fruit and Cheese Sticks

Croissants are famous for breakfast. This recipe is made with croissants, fruits, and cheese by threading them on skewers to make a healthy and delicious breakfast.

Serves 4 | Prep. time 20 minutes | Cooking time 15 minutes

Ingredients
4 small or 2 large croissants, cut into 1½-inch pieces
1 tablespoon extra-virgin olive oil
Salt, to taste
Black pepper, to taste
12 ounces cheese, cut into 1½-inch cubes
4 bananas, cut into 1½-inch pieces
16 strawberries, small
Honey, for drizzle

8 bamboo skewers

Directions
1. If using bamboo skewers, let them soak 30 minutes in water before using.
2. In a large bowl, add the croissants, olive oil, salt, and pepper; toss to combine evenly.
3. Thread the croissants onto the skewers and cook over the campfire for 10–15 minutes while rotating the skewers.
4. Remove the croissant from the skewers and let them cool.
5. Thread cheese, fruits, and croissants onto the skewers.
6. Drizzle honey over the prepared skewers and serve.

Nutrition per serving
Calories 352, fat 21 g, carbs 33 g, sugar 16 g,
Protein 13 g, sodium 448 mg

Cinnamon Roll-Ups

Cinnamon rolls are trendy, and people love to eat them. In this recipe, we made the cinnamon roll-ups on a stick by rolling the dough around the skewer and then rolling it in a cinnamon-sugar mix.

Serves 4 | Prep. time 5 minutes | Cooking time 5 minutes

Ingredients
⅛ cup sugar
½ tablespoons ground cinnamon
½ package crescent roll

4 thick wood sticks

Directions
1. If using bamboo skewers, let them soak 30 minutes in water before using.
2. In a small bowl, mix the sugar and ground cinnamon.
3. Separate the crescent rolls and wrap them around the wood sticks.
4. Roll them in the sugar and cinnamon mix.
5. Cook over the campfire for about 5 minutes while rotating.
6. Serve hot or cold with white glaze, honey, or maple syrup.

Nutrition per serving
Calories 110, fat 5 g, carbs 12 g, sugar 1 g,
Protein 0 g, sodium 15 mg

Bacon on a Stick

Did you know that 70% of all bacon in the US is eaten at breakfast time? The bacon in this recipe is made on a skewer with different seasonings.

Serves 4 | Prep. time 5 minutes | Cooking time 30 minutes

Ingredients
1 pound bacon strips
1 cup brown sugar
¾ teaspoon cayenne pepper, or to taste
1 teaspoon salt, or to taste

Skewers, either metal or bamboo

Directions
1. If using bamboo skewers, let them soak 30 minutes in water before using.
2. In a large bowl, add the bacon, sugar, pepper, and salt.
3. Rub each bacon strip in the seasoning evenly.
4. Weave each bacon strip on the skewer, leave gaps within the weave, and leave a few inches empty on the end of the skewer.
5. Prepare the campfire and set 2 rocks/logs on each side of the campfire to place the skewer on the rock/logs over the fire.
6. Put the skewers on the rock/logs and cook for about 30 minutes.
7. Rotate the skewers every 5 minutes for even cooking.
8. Serve hot with bread and eggs.

Nutrition per serving
Calories 646, fat 45 g, carbs 46 g, sugar 4 g,
Protein 14 g, sodium 763

Egg in an Orange

Eggs are a nutritious breakfast choice. In addition, they are a great source of protein. This recipe is made by just cracking the egg in an orange cup.

Serves 4 | Prep. time 5 minutes | Cooking time 10 minutes

Ingredients
4 oranges, large
4 eggs, large
Salt, to taste
Black pepper, to taste

Metal or wooden Skewers

Directions
1. If using bamboo skewers, let them soak 30 minutes in water before using.
2. Cut ⅓ of the orange top and, using a spoon, scrape out the fruit from each orange.
3. Crack 1 egg in each orange.
4. Sprinkle salt and pepper over the egg.
5. Thread a skewer on the top of each orange cup, ½ inch below the top.
6. Grasp the end of the skewer and hold the orange cups over the campfire (you can also place the skewer on the rock/logs) and let them cook for about 10 minutes.
7. Serve hot with bread.

Nutrition per serving
Calories 70, fat 5 g, carbs 0 g, sugar 0 g,
Protein 6 g, sodium 70 mg

Breakfast Campfire Biscuits Cup

Serves 4 | Prep. time 10 minutes | Cooking time 15 minutes

Ingredients
½ package refrigerated biscuit dough
4 eggs
2 strips bacon, cut in half
¼ cup milk

4 tarts on fire campfire sticks or woof'em or cobbler sticks

Directions
1. Divide the biscuit dough into 4 equal parts.
2. Stretch and flatten each biscuit dough to a flat circle in your hand.
3. Stretch one biscuit dough over one cobbler stick, and smooth out the creases. Make sure the dough is ¼-inch thick for even and quick cooking.
4. Place the biscuit dough sticks over the campfire and cook for about 5–10 minutes or until evenly browned; rotate frequently. For helpful tips on making campfire biscuit cups, go to page 4.
5. Remove the biscuit sticks from the campfire and let them cool for about 5–10 minutes before carefully removing the biscuit cups from the sticks.
6. To make the filling, fry the bacon in a skillet until crispy. Set it aside and reserve the bacon grease.
7. In a bowl, beat eggs with the milk.
8. Cook on the skillet with the bacon grease until eggs are cooked to preferred doneness.
9. Spoon eggs onto the biscuit cup and top with bacon pieces.
10. Serve.

Nutrition per serving
Calories 292, fat 16 g, carbs 25 g, sugar 3 g,
Protein 11 g, sodium 763 mg

APPETIZERS AND SIDES

Wrapped Brussels Sprouts

This recipe is made by simply wrapping the brussels sprouts in bacon strips, seasoning them with spices, and cooking them over the grill.

Serves 4 | Prep. time 10 minutes | Cooking time 10 minutes

Ingredients
1 tablespoon olive oil
⅓ cup soy sauce, low sodium
¼ teaspoon garlic, powder
½ teaspoon salt, or to taste
¼ teaspoon black pepper
16 brussels sprouts
8 slices bacon, halved to make 16 slices

Metal or bamboo skewers

Directions
1. If using bamboo skewers, let them soak 30 minutes in water before using. In a large bowl, add the olive oil, soy sauce, garlic powder, salt, and pepper.
2. Add the brussels sprouts to the soy sauce mixture; let sit for about 20 minutes.
3. Preheat the grill to medium to high.
4. Wrap each brussels sprout into a bacon slice; repeat with the rest of the Brussel sprouts.
5. Thread the skewers into the wrapped brussels sprouts.
6. Place the prepared wrapped Brussel sprouts on the grill and cook for about 5 minutes; flip and grill for another 5 minutes or until the bacon is crispy and the brussels sprouts are charred.
7. Remove from the grill and serve.

Nutrition per serving
Calories 130, fat 11 g, carbs 4 g, sugar 1 g,
Protein 5 g, sodium 706 mg

Cherry Feta Olive Salad Sticks

This is a quick salad sticks recipe made in no time by threading tomatoes, cheese, and olives on the skewers.

Serves 6 | Prep. time 10 minutes

Ingredients
9 cherry tomatoes, halved
9-ounce feta cheese block, cut into 1-inch cubes
9 black olives, pitted and cut lengthwise in 2
Salt and black pepper to taste

6 skewers, either metal or bamboo

Directions
1. Thread each skewer by alternating cherry tomato halves, cubes of feta cheese, and olive halves onto each skewer 3 times.
2. Sprinkle the skewers with salt and pepper to taste and serve.

Nutrition per serving
Calories 152, fat 11 g, carbs 2 g, sugar 2 g,
Protein 7 g, sodium 667 mg

Skewered Mushrooms

Portobello mushrooms are filled with valuable nutrients. This recipe is made by tossing the mushrooms with a marinade for added flavors of garlic and herbs and grilled.

Serves 4 | Prep. time 10 minutes | Cooking time 10 minutes

Ingredients
8 ounces brown mushrooms

Marinade
2 tablespoons olive oil
2 tablespoons soy sauce
1-1 ½ teaspoons granulated garlic or to taste
1 teaspoon dried thyme
Salt and pepper to taste

Skewers, either metal or bamboo

Directions
1. Clean the mushrooms if needed and cut them into halves
2. If using bamboo skewers, let them soak 30 minutes in water before using.
3. In a bowl mix all the marinade ingredients. Add the mushrooms and let marinate for 10-15 minutes, stirring occasionally.
4. Preheat the grill to medium to high heat.
5. Thread the skewers into the mushrooms. Keep the marinade and set it aside
6. Place the prepared skewers on the grill and cook for about 3-4 minutes on each side; flip the skewers and brush the mushrooms with the remaining marinade.
7. Remove the skewers from the grill and serve.

Nutrition per serving
Calories 54, fat 4 g, carbs 3 g, sugar 1 g,
Protein 2 g, sodium 296 mg

Crispy Accordion Potatoes

These potatoes are made with butter, garlic, and spices on the skewers over the grill.

Serves 4 | Prep. time 5 minutes | Cooking time 20 minutes

Ingredients
¼ cups butter
1 clove garlic, minced or 1 teaspoon granulated garlic
½ teaspoon salt
¼ teaspoon black pepper
4 large potatoes, whole

Heavy-duty foil
4 skewers, either metal or bamboo

Directions
1. If using bamboo skewers, let them soak 30 minutes in water before using.
2. In a small bowl, add the butter, garlic, salt, and pepper; mix well. Set aside.
3. Slice the potato crosswise, leaving ½ inch at the end still attached. Repeat with the remaining potatoes.
4. Brush the butter mixture on the potatoes evenly.
5. Double wrap the skewers with foil.
6. Place the prepared skewers over the campfire and cook for about 45 minutes or until tender and golden brown, on low to medium flame. Turn over every 10 minutes. Serve hot.

Nutrition per serving
Calories 448, fat 28 g, carbs 47 g, sugar 2 g,
Protein 6 g, sodium 236 mg

Zucchini and Smoked Salmon Rolls

This side recipe is easy and quick by rolling zucchini, salmon, and dill and cooking on the grill.

Serves 4 | Prep. time 5 minutes | Cooking time 7 minutes

Ingredients
2 zucchinis, large, cut into thin slices lengthwise (make 8 strips)
8 smoked salmon slices, cut into half
8 dill strings
1 teaspoon salt, or to taste

8 skewers, either metal or bamboo

Directions
1. If using bamboo skewers, let them soak 30 minutes in water before using.
2. Keep the remaining marinade and set aside
3. Preheat the grill to medium to high heat.
4. Place the zucchini strips on an even surface.
5. Place a smoked salmon slice on the zucchini.
6. Put the dill string in between the salmon and roll.
7. Thread the skewers into the rolled zucchini.
8. Sprinkle the zucchini rolls with salt.
9. Place the prepared skewers on the grill and cook for about 5–7 minutes; turn frequently.
10. Remove the skewers from the grill and serve.

Nutrition per serving
Calories 35, fat 1 g, carbs 6 g, sugar 3 g,
Protein 4 g, sodium 97 mg

Caprese Salad Skewers

This is a quick salad everyone will enjoy with the main course. This recipe is made by threading the tomato and cheese on the skewer, seasoning with salt, and drizzling with olive oil.

Serves 6 | Prep. time 10 minutes

Ingredients
12 cherry tomatoes
12 mozzarella cheese balls, cherry size
¼ teaspoon salt
1 tablespoon olive oil

6 skewers, either metal or bamboo

Directions
1. Thread 2 cherry tomatoes and 2 cheese balls in each skewer, alternating between the cheese and tomatoes. Repeat to prepare all the skewers.
2. Sprinkle with salt and drizzle with olive oil and then serve.

Nutrition per serving
Calories 86, fat 7 g, carbs 1 g, sugar 1 g,
Protein 4 g, sodium 57 mg

Easy Shrimp Skewers

Shrimps are very nutritious. They provide a high amount of protein. This recipe is made using shrimp with lemon and garlic by adding different seasonings.

Serves 4 | Prep. time 5 minutes | Cooking time 10 minutes

Ingredients
1 pound large shrimp, peeled and deveined
½ lemon cut into wedges

Marinade
2 tablespoons lemon juice
½ cup olive oil
¾ teaspoon salt
¼ teaspoon black pepper
1 teaspoon Italian seasonings
1 teaspoon granulated garlic

Metal or bamboo skewers

Directions
1. Take a resealable plastic bag, and add the shrimp, lemon juice, olive oil, salt, black pepper, Italian seasoning, and garlic.
2. Seal the bag; toss to coat evenly.
3. Let it sit for 15 minutes or up to 2 hours in the cooler. Do not marinate the shrimps for more than 2 hours as the acid in the lemon will start to cook the shrimp.
4. If using bamboo skewers, let them soak 30 minutes in water before using.
5. Thread the shrimp onto skewers.
6. Heat the grill over medium-high heat.
7. Place the shrimp on the grill and let each side cook for about 2-3 minutes or until the shrimp are opaque and pink.
8. Serve with lemon wedges.

Nutrition per serving
Calories 206, fat 10 g, carbs 0 g, sugar 0 g,
Protein 23 g, sodium 1,317 mg

Cuban Sandwich Sticks

This recipe is made by threading the bread, lettuce, ham, cheese, and olives onto the skewers for a quick and yummy appetizer.

Serves 6 | Prep. time 10 minutes

Ingredients
6 lettuce leaves
3 cheddar cheese slices, cut from between
6 deli ham slices
6 green olives, pitted
6 garlic bread slices

6 skewers, either metal or bamboo

Directions
1. Put lettuce, cheese, ham, and olives on the bread piece.
2. Prepare the other 5 pieces in the same order.
3. Thread a skewer from the top to the sandwich.
4. Serve with mustard and mayo if desired.

Nutrition per serving
Calories 264, fat 11 g, carbs 25 g, sugar 3 g,
Protein 13 g, sodium 979 mg

Sesame Tuna Bites

This dish is made by grilling the tuna with sesame seeds, giving you a quick and tasty appetizer.

Serves 6 | Prep. time 35 minutes | Cooking time 5 minutes

Ingredients
½ pound fresh tuna, sushi-grade, cut into 1-inch pieces
¼ cup sesame seeds, black and white
½ avocado, sliced

Marinade
2 tablespoons soy sauce
1 tablespoon sesame oil
1 tablespoon olive oil, light
½ tablespoon rice wine vinegar
½ tablespoon honey
½ teaspoon ginger, freshly minced

6 metal or bamboo skewers
Toothpicks for serving

Directions
1. If using bamboo skewers, let them soak 30 minutes in water before using.
2. In a large bowl, add the tuna, soy sauce, oils, vinegar, honey, and ginger; stir until well combined.
3. Marinate for about 20 minutes.
4. Spread sesame seeds on a plate.
5. Roll the 2 opposite sides of the tuna in the sesame seeds.
6. Thread the tuna pieces onto the skewers.
7. Grill for about 15–20 minutes on each side (the center should be pink and rare).
8. Remove from grill, and thread a tuna piece and avocado slice on a toothpick.
9. Serve with your favorite sauce or dip.

Nutrition per serving
Calories 161, fat 12 g, carbs 4 g, sugar 2 g,
Protein 10 g, sodium 287 mg

Brat Skewers

This recipe is made with bratwurst, bread, and cheese by threading onto skewers and grilling.

Serves 6 | Prep. time 20 minutes | Rest time 1 hours Cooking time 20 minutes

Ingredients
16 ounces uncooked bratwurst links, cut into 2-inch chunks
3 tablespoons brown sugar
1 teaspoon salt, or to taste
¼ teaspoon cayenne pepper
3 slices loaf bread, cut into 2 pieces each
½ cup shredded cheddar cheese

6 skewers, either metal or bamboo

Directions
1. If using bamboo skewers, let them soak 30 minutes in water before using.
2. In a large bowl, add the bratwurst, sugar, salt, and pepper.
3. Toss to combine well; let it rest for 1 hour.
4. Thread the bratwurst onto the skewers.
5. Grill for about 15–20 minutes or until the bratwurst is no longer pink while rotating frequently.
6. Remove the bratwurst from the skewers.
7. First thread bread and the bratwurst onto the skewers.
8. Sprinkle shredded cheese over the bread and bratwurst.
9. Grill for 2-3 minutes, bread side on the grill, and serve hot.

Nutrition per serving
Calories 137, fat 9 g, carbs 17 g, sugar 5 g,
Protein 9 g, sodium 377

CHICKEN

Smoked Rotisserie Chicken

This recipe requires brining the chickens at home overnight and cooking them at the campsite on a spit rotisserie over the campfire to get the most delicious smoky flavors and very juicy chickens.

Serves 8 | Prep. time 20 minutes | Cooking time 240 minutes

Ingredients
Brine
1 cup salt
1 cup sugar
1 gallon water

Other ingredients
2 whole chickens, about 3 ½ pounds each
2 cups apple cider vinegar
1 teaspoon salt and pepper
¼ cup brown sugar
1 (12-ounce) beer
Barbecue sauce for serving, optional

Equipment
Battery-powered spit rotisserie with vertical support rods
Instant-read meat thermometer
Spray bottle

Directions
1. At home, prepare the brine. In a large stockpot, add the 2 chickens, salt, sugar, and a gallon of water to cover the chickens. Let it rest for about 4-5 hours or overnight in the refrigerator. To bring to the campsite, remove the chicken from the marinade, and pat dry with kitchen towels.
2. Truss your chickens by attaching the legs and the wings tightly together with kitchen twine.

3. Store both chickens in an airtight container or large resealable plastic bag and place in the cooler until ready to use.
4. Prepare the rotisserie over the campfire. The chicken should not touch the campfire flames and should be set about 4 inches just above the flames.
5. Light the campfire and keep it going as much as you can at the same temperature by adding wood regularly while the chickens are cooking.
6. Thread the chickens tightly onto the rotisserie stick. Start the rotisserie. Make sure to have extra batteries in case it's needed.
7. In a spray bottle, add the apple cider vinegar, salt and pepper, brown sugar, and beer. Spray generously the chickens on all sides with this mixture and continue spraying regularly while the chicken is cooking, every 30 minutes.
8. Cook the chickens for about 4 to 6 hours or until the internal temperature at the chicken's meaty thickest part reaches 165°F (74°C) on the instant-read meat thermometer.
9. Warm the barbecue sauce if desired and serve with the chicken.

Nutrition per serving
Calories 247, fat 11 g, carbs 13 g, sugar 12 g,
Protein 24 g, sodium 624 mg

Peruvian Chicken Skewer

These Peruvian chicken skewers are made with chicken thigh cubes, seasoned with different spices, and served with crushed peanuts.

Serves 6 | Prep. time 20 minutes | Marinating time 30 minutes Cooking time 20 minutes

Ingredients
3 pounds chicken thighs, skinless and boneless
Crushed peanuts for serving, optional

Marinade
3 garlic cloves, minced
1 teaspoon chili powder
1 teaspoon ground cumin
½ teaspoon red pepper flakes, crushed
1 teaspoon smoked paprika
2 tablespoons brown sugar
2 tablespoons extra-virgin olive oil
2 tablespoons soy sauce
2 tablespoons lime juice, fresh
2 tablespoons fresh ginger, minced

Skewers, either metal or bamboo

Directions
1. Prepare the marinate at home. In a large bowl, mix all the marinade ingredients until well combined. Place in an airtight container.
2. At the campsite, cut the excess fat from the chicken and cut it into 1-inch pieces.
3. Reserve half the marinade for later use and add the chicken in the other half, toss to coat evenly, and let it sit for about 30 minutes.
4. Oil the grate and prepare the campfire or barbecue grill for a medium to high heat.
5. If using bamboo skewers, let them soak 30 minutes in water before using.
6. Thread the chicken pieces onto the skewers.

7. Put the chicken skewers on the grate and cook for about 13–15 minutes; turn every 3-4 minutes until golden brown.
8. Brush on the remaining marinade and cook for another 2-3 minutes.
9. Remove the chicken skewers from the grill and wrap them with the foil; let rest for 5-10 minutes.
10. Sprinkle the peanuts and serve.

Nutrition per serving
Calories 366, fat 14 g, carbs 5 g, sugar 4 g,
Protein 51 g, sodium 454 mg

BBQ Chicken Skewers

Barbeques are popular everywhere. These barbeque skewers are made with chicken breasts, veggies, and spices over the grill.

Serves 4 | Prep. time 10 minutes | Cooking time 15 minutes

Ingredients
6 bell peppers, medium, cut into thick pieces
1 onion, large, cut into thick pieces
⅛ cup chili powder
½ tablespoon paprika
¼ teaspoon ground thyme
1 teaspoon garlic powder
½ teaspoon cumin powder
⅛ teaspoon cayenne pepper
½ tablespoon brown sugar
1 tablespoon olive oil
1 teaspoon salt, or to taste
¼ teaspoon black pepper
2 chicken breasts, boneless

4–6 skewers, either metal or bamboo

Directions
1. If using bamboo skewers, let them soak 30 minutes in water before using.
2. In a large bowl, add the bell peppers, onion, chili powder, paprika, thyme, garlic, cumin, cayenne pepper, sugar, oil, salt, and black pepper; mix well.
3. Add the chicken into the seasoning mix bowl, and toss to coat evenly.
4. Let it sit for about 10 minutes.
5. Thread the chicken, peppers, and onions until the skewers are full repeatedly.
6. Preheat the grill from medium to high.
7. Place the prepared skewers on the grill and cook for about 10–15 minutes or until chicken and vegetables are tender; rotate frequently.
8. Serve hot with your favorite sauce or dip.

Nutrition per serving
Calories 121, fat 7 g, carbs 9 g, sugar 5 g,
Protein 7 g, sodium 605 mg

Mexican Chicken Skewers

Chicken cooked on the grill is tempting as well as tasty, made using juices, spices, garlic, and sauce.

Serves 6 | Prep. time 15 minutes | Marinating time 4 hours Cooking time 20 minutes

Ingredients
12 chicken thighs boneless and skinless, cut into halves lengthwise

Marinade
1 cup orange juice
½ cup lime juice
¼ cup vegetable oil
3 tablespoons chili powder
3-4 garlic cloves, coarsely chopped
Salt and black pepper, to taste
2 tablespoons chipotle in adobo sauce

6 skewers, either metal or bamboo

Directions
1. At home, prepare the marinade by all the marinade ingredients to a large bowl; mix well. Transfer to an airtight container large enough to add the chicken at the campsite or use a large resealable plastic bag.
2. At the campsite, add the chicken to the marinade for at least 4 hours in the cooler.
3. Prepare the grill to high heat.
4. If using bamboo skewers, let them soak 30 minutes in water before using.
5. Thread the skewer onto the chicken and grill for 7-10 minutes on each side or until the chicken is tender and cooked through.
6. Remove the chicken skewers from the grill and let them rest for 5 minutes before serving.

Nutrition per serving
Calories 112, fat 5 g, carbs 2 g, sugar 1 g,
Protein 14 g, sodium 212 mg

Piri Piri Chicken Sticks

Sometime simple is best! This recipe is made using boneless chicken breasts on skewers over the grill with piri piri seasoning.

Serves 4 | Prep. time 10 minutes | Resting time 30 minutes Cooking time 30 minutes

Ingredients
4 chicken breasts, boneless and skinless
2 tablespoons piri piri seasoning

Skewers, either metal or bamboo

Directions
1. Wash the chicken with water and pat dry. Cut chicken into long strips
2. In a large bowl, add the chicken and piri piri seasoning and toss to coat evenly. Let it sit for about 30 minutes.
3. Preheat the grill to medium heat.
4. If using bamboo skewers, let them soak 30 minutes in water before using.
5. Thread the chicken onto the skewers.
6. Place the chicken skewers on the grill and let them cook for about 10-15 minutes on each side or until cooked through and internal temperature reaches 165°F (74°C) on an instant-read meat thermometer.
7. Let rest 5-10 minutes before serving

Nutrition per serving
Calories 218, fat 10 g, carbs 3 g, sugar 2 g,
Protein 27 g, sodium 687 mg

Salsa Chicken Sticks

Salsa chicken sticks are made on skewers using chicken, salsa, and seasonings over the grill.

Serves 4 | Prep. time 10 minutes | Marinating time 2–24 hours Cooking time 10 minutes

Ingredients
Marinade
2 tablespoons medium or hot salsa
4 cloves garlic, minced
½ tablespoon olive oil
¼ teaspoon lemon pepper seasoning
½ teaspoon poultry seasoning

Other ingredients
1 pound chicken breasts, cut into strips
¼ cup medium salsa, plus more for serving

Skewers, either metal or bamboo

Directions
1. At home, prepare the marinade in a large bowl, mix well to combine. Transfer to an airtight container (large enough to add the chicken at the campsite) or use a large resealable plastic bag.
2. At the campsite, add the chicken to the salsa mixture, toss to coat evenly, and let it marinate for 2 hours to 24 hours. Place in the cooler.
3. Prepare the grill to medium heat.
4. Thread the prepared chicken onto the skewers.
5. If using bamboo skewers, let them soak 30 minutes in water before using.
6. Place the prepared skewers on the grill and cook for about 9–10 minutes, or until the chicken is no longer pink and cook through.
7. Flip over after 5 minutes
8. Brush the ¼ cup of salsa on the chicken during the last 2 minutes of grilling.
9. Serve hot with extra salsa for dipping.

Nutrition per serving
Calories 148, fat 3 g, carbs 2 g, sugar 1 g,
Protein 27 g, sodium 271 mg

Campfire Biscuit Cups with BBQ Chicken

These campfire biscuit cups are filled with chicken and zucchini coated in barbecue sauce making this an all-time favorite without and dishes to make.

Serves 4 | Prep. time 10 minutes | Cooking time 15 minutes

Ingredients
1 ½ cups leftover cooked chicken, shredded
1 zucchini, trimmed and diced
½ cup bottled BBQ sauce
1 package refrigerated biscuit dough

8 tarts on fire campfire sticks or woof'em or cobbler sticks

Directions
1. In a bowl mix, the zucchini and shredded chicken. Mix in the BBQ sauce until well combined. Transfer chicken mixture to a triple layer of heavy-duty foil.
2. Fold the packet seal tightly, leaving some space over the mixture.
3. Place on the side of the campfire, turning a few times to even out the heat.
4. Let cook for 10-15 minutes or until warmed through.
5. Divide the biscuit dough into 8 equal parts.
6. Stretch and flatten each biscuit dough to a flat circle in your hand.
7. Stretch one biscuit dough over one cobbler stick, and smooth out the creases. Make sure the dough is ¼-inch thick for even and quick cooking.
8. Place the biscuit dough sticks over the campfire and cook for about 5–10 minutes or until evenly browned; rotate frequently. For helpful tips on making campfire biscuit cups, go to page 4.
9. Remove the biscuit sticks from the campfire and let them cool for about 5–10 minutes before carefully removing the biscuit cups from the sticks.

10. Once the chicken is warmed, open the packet carefully and spoon evenly the filling into each cooked biscuit cup and serve.

Nutrition per serving
Calories 558, fat 49 g, carbs 24 g, sugar 3 g,
Protein 6 g, sodium 916 mg

BEEF, PORK, AND LAMB

Steak on a Stick

Steaks are loved. This is a juicy steak recipe made using flank steak, spices, soy sauce, ginger, and garlic over the grill.

Serves 6 | Prep. time 10 minutes | Marinating time 4 hours Cooking time 10 minutes

Ingredients
2 pounds flank steak, cut into strips
Sesame seeds, for serving, optional

Marinade
½ cup soy sauce
¼ cup olive oil
¼ cup water
2 tablespoons molasses
2 teaspoons mustard powder
1 teaspoon ginger powder
½ teaspoons garlic powder
½ teaspoons onion powder

Skewers, either metal or bamboo

Directions
1. In a large bowl, prepare the marinade by adding all the marinade ingredient in a bowl and mixing until well combined. **Transfer to an airtight container (large enough to add the chicken at the campsite) or use a large resealable plastic bag.**
2. At the campsite, add the steak to the marinade and toss to evenly combine. Let it rest for at least 4 hours in the cooler.
3. Preheat the barbecue to medium to high heat.
4. If using bamboo skewers, let them soak 30 minutes in water before using.
5. Thread the steak strips onto the skewers.
6. Place the prepared skewers on the grill and cook for 4-5 minutes on each side.

7. Sprinkle the sesame seeds and serve.

Nutrition per serving
Calories 660, fat 40 g, carbs 13 g, sugar 8 g,
Protein 61 g, sodium 2,318 mg

Beef Kabobs

These kabobs are made with sirloin steak, tomato paste, spice, and peanut butter by threading them on skewers and cooking over the grill.

Serves 4 | Prep. time 10 minutes | Marinating time 20 minutes Cooking time 15 minutes

Ingredients
1 pound sirloin steak, cut into 1-inch pieces
1 small onion, diced
2 tablespoons peanut butter, creamy
1 tablespoon tomato, paste
1 tablespoon olive oil
2 teaspoons allspice
Salt and black pepper to taste
Cooking spray

Skewers, either metal or bamboo

Directions
1. If using bamboo skewers, let them soak 30 minutes in water before using.
2. In a large bowl, add the steak, onion, peanut butter, tomato paste, oil, allspice, salt, and pepper. Toss to combine well. Let it sit for 20 minutes.
3. Oil the BBQ grate.
4. Prepare the grill to medium to high heat.
5. Thread the steak onto the skewers.
6. Place the prepared skewers on the grill and cook for about 10–15 minutes or until the meat is browned, flipping while cooking.
7. Remove the beef skewers from the grill and serve hot.

Nutrition per serving
Calories 249, fat 13 g, carbs 6 g, sugar 2 g,
Protein 27 g, sodium 428 mg

Hot Dog Wrapped in Dough

This is simple but delicious, made by threading the hot dogs and cheese on the skewers and wrapping them with dough.

Serves 6 | Prep. time 10 minutes | Cooking time 20 minutes

Ingredients
6 hot dogs
3 sticks string cheese, cut into thin strips
1 can pizza dough, cut 1-inch slices lengthwise
Ketchup, mayonnaise, mustard for serving

6 skewers, either metal or bamboo
Heavy-duty foil

Directions
1. If using bamboo skewers, let them soak 30 minutes in water before using.
2. Thread a skewer into each hot dog.
3. Cut the spiral but hold the knife diagonally to the top of the hot dog and roll it down until you reach the bottom.
4. Wind the cheese strip into the spiral groove on each hot dog; fill the entire spiral.
5. Roll the pizza dough around the hot dog; make sure that the dough overlaps so the cheese won't leak through.
6. Loosely wrap the hot dogs in the foil so the dough has space to expand.
7. Place the hot dogs over the campfire, let them cook for about 10 minutes, check if the dough is puffed, and then flip the hot dogs and cook for another 10 minutes.
8. Let the hot dogs cool before unwrapping.
9. Serve with ketchup, mustard, and mayonnaise, as desired

Nutrition per serving
Calories 479, fat 24 g, carbs 50 g, sugar 10 g,
Protein 14 g, sodium 699 mg

Cumin Lamb Skewers

This recipe is made by tossing the lamb with different spices and oil and then threading it on the skewers and cooking over the grill.

Serves 6 | Prep. time 30 minutes | Cooking time 15 minutes

Ingredients
1 tablespoon red chili flakes, crushed
1 tablespoon cumin seeds, ground
2 teaspoons fennel seeds, ground
1 teaspoon salt, or to taste
2 teaspoons garlic, minced
1 tablespoon vegetable/canola oil
2 teaspoons Shaoxing wine, optional
2 teaspoons water
2 pounds lamb shoulder, boneless, cut into 1-inch pieces

Directions
1. If using bamboo skewers, let them soak 30 minutes in water before using.
2. In a medium bowl, add the red chili flakes, cumin, fennel, salt, and garlic; mix well.
3. Reserve 1 tablespoon of the cumin mix.
4. Add the oil and wine/water to the cumin spices mix; mix well. Add the lamb into the cumin mixture; toss to coat evenly.
5. Thread the lamb onto the skewer tightly, leaving no space in between except a 3-inch margin at the bottom of the skewer.
6. Preheat the grill for 5 minutes to medium to high.
7. Brush the grill with oil.
8. Place the lamb skewers on the grill and let them cook for about 4-5 minutes on each side.
9. Rotate while grilling, sprinkle the reserved cumin spices, and cook for another 1 minute.
10. Remove the lamb skewers from the grill and serve hot.

Nutrition per serving
Calories 175, fat 8 g, carbs 2 g, sugar 0 g,
Protein 23 g, sodium 238 mg

Grilled Teriyaki Pork

Teriyaki grills are famous. This recipe is made by tossing the pork pieces with fruit juice, soy sauce, brown sugar, ginger, and garlic and cooking over the grill.

Serves 4 | Prep. time 10 minutes | Marinating time 60 minutes Cooking time 15 minutes

Ingredients
2 pounds pork loin roast, cut into 1-inch pieces
¾ cup soy sauce
¾ cup brown sugar
½ cup pineapple juice
2 cloves garlic, minced
½ teaspoon ginger, minced
Salad for serving, optional

8 skewers

Directions
1. In a large bowl, add the first 6 ingredients, stir to coat the pork pieces evenly, and let sit for at least 60 minutes.
2. If using bamboo skewers, let them soak 30 minutes in water before using.
3. Preheat the grill to medium to high.
4. Thread the pork onto the skewers.
5. Place the pork on the grill and cook for about 3–5 minutes on each side.
6. Remove from the grill and serve with salad.

Nutrition per serving
Calories 502, fat 10 g, carbs 48 g, sugar 44 g,
Protein 56, sodium 2,554 mg

Filipino BBQ Pork

In this recipe, pork is made in a BBQ way by simply combing spices, soda, sugar, vinegar, ketchup, and garlic.

Serves 4 | Prep. time 20 minutes | Cooking time 20 minutes

Ingredients
1½ pounds pork shoulder, boneless, cut into 1-inch pieces
Rice or salad for serving

Marinade
¼ cup banana ketchup
½ cup soy sauce
½ cup lime lemon or lime soda such as 7UP and Sprite
⅛ cup oyster sauce
¼ cup white vinegar
1 tablespoon chili oil with black bean
½ cup brown sugar
1 teaspoon black pepper, ground
½ cups garlic, minced

8 skewers, either metal or bamboo

Directions
1. At home, prepare the marinade by mixing all the marinade ingredients in a bowl.
2. Mix until the sugar is dissolved, and all ingredients are well combined. Transfer to an airtight container large enough to add the pork or use a large plastic resealable bag.
3. At the campsite, add the pork to the marinade and let it sit for 6 hours but not more than 8 hours in the cooler.
4. Preheat the grill to medium to high.
5. If using bamboo skewers, let them soak 30 minutes in water before using.
6. Thread the pork pieces onto the skewers. Keep the marinade for basting.
7. Place the prepared skewers on the grill and cook for about 4-5 minutes on each side.

8. Brush the pork with the remaining marinade and cook for another 1 minute on each side or until the pork is well glazed.
9. Serve with rice or salad.

Nutrition per serving
Calories 187, fat 6 g, carbs 21 g, sugar 16 g,
Protein 13 g, sodium 1,062 mg

Morocco Kofta Balls

These kofta balls are made with ground beef or lamb, combined with spices, herbs, and onion, cooked over the grill.

Serves 4 | Prep. time 20 minutes | Cooking time 10 minutes

Ingredients
1 pound ground beef or lamb or combine the two
1 medium onion, finely chopped
2 teaspoons paprika
1 teaspoon cumin, ground
1 teaspoon salt
¼ teaspoon black pepper
⅛ teaspoon cayenne pepper
¼ cup fresh parsley, chopped
¼ cup fresh cilantro, chopped
1 teaspoon ground cinnamon, optional
1 teaspoon fresh mint leaves for serving
1 teaspoon crushed dry chili for serving

Skewers, either metal or bamboo

Directions
1. At home, in a large bowl, add the first 10 ingredients, and combine well. Transfer to an airtight container. Let sit for about 1 hour or longer in the refrigerator or at room temperature.
2. At the campsite, preheat the grill to medium to high.
3. If using bamboo skewers, let them soak 30 minutes in water before using.
4. Take a small amount of the kofta mixture and make it into a cylinder shape. Thread the skewers into the prepared kofta carefully; do not break any.
5. Place the prepared skewers on the grill and cook for about 5-6 minutes on each side or until cooked through.
6. Sprinkle mint leaves and dry red chili on the koftas if desired and serve.

Nutrition per serving
Calories 326, fat 20 g, carbs 4 g, sugar 1 g,
Protein 31 g, sodium 637 mg

Grilled Hawaiian Steak Skewers

These steak skewers are made with veggies, fruit juice, soy sauce, ketchup, brown sugar, and more.

Serves 4 | Prep. time 10 minutes | Cooking time 15 minutes

Ingredients
2 pounds steak, cut into 2-inch pieces
1 red bell pepper, large, cut into 2-inch pieces
1 white onion, large, cut into 2-inch pieces
½ cup soy sauce
1 cup pineapple juice
1 tablespoon ketchup
1 tablespoon ginger, freshly grated
1 tablespoon garlic powder
1 cup brown sugar
Skewers, either metal or bamboo

Directions
1. In a large bowl, add all the ingredients; toss to combine evenly. Let the mixture rest for about 10–15 minutes.
2. If using bamboo skewers, let them soak 30 minutes in water before using.
3. Thread the skewer into the steak, then bell pepper, then meat, and then onion. Follow the same order to prepare the other skewers. Keep the marinade.
4. Grill for about 4–6 minutes, flip, and cook for another 4–6 minutes.
5. While the skewers are cooking, in a small saucepan, add the marinade and let boil for a few minutes until the sauce thickens. Remove from heat.
6. Serve hot with the sauce.

Nutrition per serving
Calories 742, fat 32 g, carbs 65 g, sugar 60 g,
Protein 49 g, sodium 1,790 mg

Grilled Pork Chops

Grilled pork chops are made on skewers with different spices and sauce over the grill.

Serves 6 | Prep. time 10 minutes | Cooking time 30 minutes

Ingredients
1 teaspoon paprika
1 teaspoon brown sugar
½ teaspoon onion salt
¼ teaspoon garlic, powder
¼ teaspoon ginger, powder
¼ teaspoon cinnamon, ground
¼ teaspoon cumin, ground
¼ teaspoon dry mustard
¼ teaspoon cayenne pepper
¼ teaspoon black pepper, cracked
6 boneless pork top loin chops, cut 1½-inch thick
1 tablespoon soy sauce

6 skewers, either metal or bamboo

Directions
1. At home, prepare the seasoning mix by adding to a bowl the paprika, brown sugar, onion salt, garlic, ginger, cinnamon, cumin, mustard, cayenne pepper, and black pepper. Mix well and transfer to an airtight container.
2. At the campsite, brush the soy sauce on both sides of each pork.
3. Sprinkle the mixed seasoning on the pork and rub with your fingers.
4. Preheat the grill to medium heat.
5. If using bamboo skewers, let them soak 30 minutes in water before using.
6. Thread the skewer into each pork piece.
7. Place the prepared skewers on the grill and cook for about 30–35 minutes or until chops are slightly pink and juicy; flip over every 5–7 minutes.
8. Remove the chops from the grill, let them cool for 5 minutes before serving.

Nutrition per serving
Calories 291, fat 15 g, carbs 2 g, sugar 1 g,
Protein 36 g, sodium 343 mg

Pizza Campfire Biscuit Cups

The easiest pizza you will ever make where all the ingredients are nicely tucked in a biscuit cup! Everyone will love these. Make more, you will need it.

Serves 4 | Prep. time 15 minutes | Cooking time 15 minutes

Ingredients
1 package refrigerated biscuit dough
¾ cup pizza sauce
½ cup mini pepperoni slices
½ ounce ground sausage, cooked and drained
1 cup shredded mozzarella cheese, more if needed

Tarts on fire campfire sticks or woof'em or cobbler sticks

Directions
1. Divide the biscuit dough into 8 equal parts.
2. Stretch and flatten each biscuit dough to a flat circle in your hand.
3. Stretch one biscuit dough over one cobbler stick, and smooth out the creases. Make sure the dough is ¼-inch thick for even and quick cooking.
4. Place the biscuit dough sticks over the campfire and cook for about 5–10 minutes or until evenly browned; rotate frequently. For helpful tips on making campfire biscuit cups, go to page 4.
5. Remove the biscuit sticks from the campfire and let them cool for about 5–10 minutes before carefully removing the biscuit cups from the sticks.
6. In a bowl, mix sauce, pepperoni, sauce, and ¼ of the cheese.
7. Spoon about 2 tablespoons of mixture into a cup.
8. Place a sheet of heavy-duty foil over a fire grate and arrange the biscuit cups on it. Cook for a few minutes until the cheese has melted.
9. Serve warm.

Nutrition per serving
Calories 375, fat 15 g, carbs 39 g, sugar 6 g,
Protein 12 g, sodium 854 mg

Sausage Skewers

These are cooked over the grill by threading sausages and veggies on skewers.

Serves 4 | Prep. time 20 minutes | Cooking time 12 minutes

Ingredients
19 ounces hot Italian sausage, cut into 1-inch pieces
1 large red bell pepper, cut into 1-inch pieces
1 large yellow bell pepper, cut into 1-inch pieces
1 green bell pepper, large, cut into 1-inch pieces
1 white onion, large, cut into 1-inch pieces
1 tablespoon olive oil
3 tablespoons honey mustard sauce, plus more for serving

Skewers, either metal or bamboo

Directions
1. Preheat the grill to medium to high heat.
2. In a large bowl, add all the ingredients; toss to combine well.
3. If using bamboo skewers, let them soak 30 minutes in water before using.
4. Thread skewers into a sausage piece, then onion, then another sausage piece, then green pepper, then sausage piece, then yellow pepper, then sausage, then red pepper, and sausage piece.
5. Place the prepared skewers on the grill and cook for about 12 minutes; turn every 3 minutes.
6. Remove the sausage skewers from the grill and serve them hot with honey mustard dipping sauce.

Nutrition per serving
Calories 495, fat 37 g, carbs 13 g, sugar 6 g,
Protein 27 g, sodium 1,003 mg

SEAFOOD

Fish on a Stick

These fish sticks are made with white fish, spices, herbs, and sauce on skewers over the grill.

Serves 4 | Prep. time 20 minutes | Cooking time 10 minutes

Ingredients
18 ounces white fish, cod, or other lean, cut into 12 equal pieces
¼ teaspoon salt
¼ teaspoon black pepper, ground
½ cup sesame seeds
1 tablespoon parsley, chopped
2 teaspoons lemon rind, grated
1 tablespoon olive oil
Cooking spray
½ cup tzatziki sauce, for serving, optional

Skewers, either metal or bamboo

Directions
1. Preheat the grill over medium heat.
2. If using bamboo skewers, let them soak 30 minutes in water before using.
3. Thread each skewer into 3 fish pieces.
4. Sprinkle salt and pepper on the fish.
5. In a large dish, add the sesame seeds, parsley, and lemon rind; mix.
6. Brush the fish with oil.
7. Coat the fish skewers with the seeds mix evenly.
8. Spray the cooking oil on the fish.
9. Place the fish on the grill and cook for about 2-3 minutes on each side or until the seeds are brown and the fish is firm.
10. Serve with the tzatziki.

Nutrition per serving
Calories 263, fat 17 g, carbs 5 g, sugar 0 g,
Protein 23 g, sodium 324 mg

Grilled Garlic Shrimp

Shrimps are high in nutrition. These shrimps are made over the grill with butter, herb, garlic, and salt.

Serves 4 | Prep. time 15 minutes | Cooking time 25 minutes

Ingredients
1 pound large shrimp, peeled and deveined
Extra-virgin olive oil
¼ teaspoon kosher salt
3 tablespoons garlic butter, at room temperature

Skewers, either metal or bamboo

Directions
1. If using bamboo skewers, let them soak 30 minutes in water before using.
2. Preheat the grill to high heat on the side of the grill with no coals.
3. Thread the skewer into the shrimps.
4. Brush the shrimps with olive oil, and sprinkle with salt.
5. Place the prepared skewers on the grill and cook for about 2 minutes on each side.
6. Remove the shrimps from the grill and immediately brush them with the garlic butter and serve.

Nutrition per serving
Calories 175, fat 11 g, carbs 2 g, sugar 0 g,
Protein 16 g, sodium 722 mg

Teriyaki Tuna Skewers

Tuna is a powerhouse of essential nutrients. These tuna skewers are made by marinade with teriyaki sauce, oil, ginger, and garlic rolled in sesame seeds.

Serves 4 | Prep. time 20 minutes | Marinating time 30 minutes Cooking time 4 minutes

Ingredients
2 pounds fresh tuna steak, cut into 1-inch pieces
1 tablespoon sesame seeds, toasted, for garnish

Marinade
2 cups teriyaki sauce
3 ounces sesame oil
1 tablespoon ginger, freshly minced
1 teaspoon garlic, freshly minced
1 lemon juice
1 tablespoon brown sugar

Skewers, either metal or bamboo

Directions
1. At home, mix the marinade ingredient in a a bowl. Transfer to an airtight container or plastic resealable bag.
2. At the campsite, add the tuna to the marinade, seal, and place in the cooler for 30 minutes.
3. If using bamboo skewers, let them soak 30 minutes in water before using.
4. Preheat the grill to high heat.
5. Thread the skewers into the tuna.
6. Place the prepared skewers on the grill and cook for about 3-4 minutes; turn frequently or until desired doneness.
7. Remove the tuna from the grill, sprinkle the sesame seeds, and serve.

Nutrition per serving
Calories 336, fat 9 g, carbs 4 g, sugar 4 g,
Protein 68 g, sodium 1,906 mg

Tuna Kebabs with Herbs, Lemon, and Grains

These kebabs are made with lemon juice and different herbs and spices over the grill.

Serves 4 | Prep. time 10 minutes | Cooking time 4 minutes

Ingredients
1 pound tuna steak, cut into 2-inch pieces
2 tablespoons harissa
2 large lemons, juiced
2½ cups toasted mixed grains, for serving, optional
1 teaspoon cumin, toasted and crushed, optional
6 onion springs, finely chopped, optional
½ medium cucumber, diced, optional
Small handful mint, chopped, optional
Small handful flat-leaf parsley, chopped, optional
8 tablespoons yogurt, optional

4 skewers, either metal or bamboo

Directions
1. In a large bowl, add the tuna, 1 lemon juice, and harissa; toss to mix well. Let it sit for about 10 minutes.
2. In the large bowl, add the grains, cumin, spring onions, and 1 lemon juice.
3. If using bamboo skewers, let them soak 30 minutes in water before using.
4. Preheat the grill to medium heat.
5. Thread the skewers into the tuna and grill for about 2-3 minutes on each side.
6. Remove the tuna from the grill and serve with the grains and yogurt if desired.

Nutrition per serving
Calories 451, fat 10 g, carbs 44 g, sugar 8 g,
Protein 43 g, sodium 626 mg

Campfire Biscuit Cups with Shrimp Salad Filling

Serves 4 | Prep. time 10 minutes | Cooking time 15 minutes

Ingredients
Shrimp filling
2 (4-ounce) can tiny shrimp
1 celery stalk, diced thin
4-6 small, sweet pickles, diced thin
1 cup mayonnaise
1 package refrigerated biscuit dough

Tarts on fire campfire sticks or woof'em or cobbler sticks

Directions
1. To make the filling, mix all ingredients in a bowl. Store in an airtight container and keep chilled.
2. Divide the biscuit dough into 8 equal parts.
3. Stretch and flatten each biscuit dough to a flat circle in your hand.
4. Stretch one biscuit dough over one cobbler stick, and smooth out the creases. Make sure the dough is ¼-inch thick for even and quick cooking.
5. Place the biscuit dough sticks over the campfire and cook for about 5–10 minutes or until evenly browned; rotate frequently. For helpful tips on making campfire biscuit cups, go to page 4.
6. Remove the biscuit sticks from the campfire and let them cool for about 5–10 minutes before carefully removing the biscuit cups from the sticks.
7. Spoon the filling into the cooked biscuit cup.
8. Serve.

Nutrition per serving
Calories 558, fat 49 g, carbs 24 g, sugar 3 g,
Protein 6 g, sodium 916 mg

VEGETARIAN

Cheesy Eggplant Skewers

These skewers are made by rolling eggplant strips with cheese, nuts, and leafy greens and cooking over the grill.

Serves 4 | Prep. time 15 minutes | Cooking time 8 minutes

Ingredients
4 long eggplants, medium, cut ½ inches thin lengthwise
4 tablespoons extra-virgin olive oil
Salt, to taste
Black pepper, to taste
½ cups ricotta cheese
1 cup walnuts
A small handful of any leafy green

Skewers, either metal or bamboo

Directions
1. If using bamboo skewers, let them soak 30 minutes in water before using.
2. Preheat the grill pan to high heat.
3. Brush oil on both sides of the eggplant and sprinkle with salt and pepper.
4. Thread the skewer onto the eggplant carefully.
5. Place the eggplants on the grill and cook for about 3-4 minutes on each side.
6. Remove the eggplants from the skewers and put them on an even surface.
7. Put the ricotta cheese on the eggplants, then walnuts, and then greens. Roll the eggplants and thread 3 rolls on each skewer from where the rolling ends and serve.

Nutrition per serving
Calories 539, fat 35 g, carbs 50 g, sugar 19 g,
Protein 12 g, sodium 39 mg

Corn With Butter and Herbs

Corns are super tasty, and cooking them with butter and herbs enhances their flavor. These corns are simply made with butter and herbs over the grill.

Serves 6 | Prep. time 5 minutes | Cooking time 24 minutes

Ingredients
½ cup unsalted butter, softened
1 teaspoon salt, or to taste
½ teaspoon black pepper, ground
½ teaspoon paprika
2 tablespoons fresh parsley, minced
6 fresh corn ears, peeled and silk removed, cut into 3 pieces each

Skewers, either metal or bamboo

Directions
1. If using bamboo skewers, let them soak 30 minutes in water before using.
2. Preheat the grill to medium to high heat.
3. In a small bowl, add the butter, salt, pepper, paprika, and parsley, mix well, and then set aside.
4. Thread the skewers into the corn.
5. Place the corn skewers on the grill and cook for about 8–12 minutes on each side or until the corn is tender.
6. Remove the skewers from the grill.
7. Immediately spread the herb butter all over the grilled corn and serve hot.

Nutrition per serving
Calories 138, fat 15 g, carbs 1 g, sugar 1 g,
Protein 1 g, sodium 391 mg

Zucchini and Cherry Skewers

This recipe is made by wrapping cheese in zucchini strips, threading zucchini and cherry tomato on the skewers, and cooking over the grill.

Serves 4 | Prep. time 15 minutes | Cooking time 5 minutes

Ingredients
2 zucchinis, large, halved, and cut into thin slices
6-ounce feta cheese block, cut into 1-inch cubes
12 cherry tomatoes
1½ teaspoons oregano, dried
½ teaspoon salt
¼ teaspoon black pepper, ground
1 tablespoon olive oil

Skewers, either metal or bamboo

Directions
1. If using bamboo skewers, let them soak 30 minutes in water before using.
2. Preheat the grill to medium heat.
3. Place the zucchini slices on the even surface, put the feta cheese on the zucchini, and fold. Repeat and make 12 cubes.
4. Thread the zucchini feta fold onto the skewer, then thread a cherry tomato, and repeat: 3 cherry tomatoes and 3 zucchini feta folds on each skewer.
5. In a small bowl, add the oregano, salt, and pepper.
6. Sprinkle the oregano mixture on the prepared skewers.
7. Place the prepared skewers on the grill and cook for about 6–8 minutes on each side or until slightly cooked; turn frequently.
8. Remove the skewers from the grill and serve hot.

Nutrition per serving
Calories 179, fat 13 g, carbs 9 g, sugar 4 g,
Protein 8.7 g, sodium 730 mg

Ratatouille Kebabs

These kebabs are made with different vegetables, spices, and oil and cooked on the grill.

Serves 4 | Prep. time 5 minutes | Cooking time 20 minutes

Ingredients
1 white onion, large, cut into 1-inch pieces
1 large red bell pepper, cut into 1-inch pieces
1 large yellow bell pepper, cut into 1-inch pieces
1 zucchini, large cut into ½-inch slices
1 yellow squash, large, cut into ½-inch slices
10 ounces baby portobello mushrooms
2 tablespoons oil
Salt, to taste
Pepper, to taste
Red pepper flakes, optional
Skewers, either metal or bamboo

Directions
1. If using bamboo skewers, let them soak 30 minutes in water before using.
2. Preheat the grill to medium to high heat.
3. Assemble your kebabs by threading the vegetables onto the skewers.
4. Brush the oil on the skewers and sprinkle with salt, pepper, and chili flakes.
5. Place the kebabs on the grill and cook for about 20 minutes or until vegetables are tender; rotate frequently.
6. Remove from the heat and serve warm.

Nutrition per serving
Calories 95, fat 1 g, carbs 30 g, sugar 8 g,
Protein 5 g, sodium 46 mg

Rainbow Veggie Skewers

These rainbow skewers are made with different vegetables coated with vinegar, herbs, and spices and cooked on the grill.

Serves 4 | Prep. time 30 minutes | Cooking time 15 minutes

Ingredients
4 red onions, medium, cut into ½-inch thick pieces
4 zucchinis, medium, cut into ½-inch thick pieces
2 yellow bell pepper, medium, cut into 1-inch pieces
2 tomatoes, large, cut into ½-inch-thick pieces
12 portobello mushrooms, medium

Balsamic sauce
3 tablespoons olive oil
2 tablespoons balsamic vinegar
5 cloves garlic, minced
3 tablespoons parsley, minced
3 tablespoons cilantro, minced
1 teaspoon rosemary, minced
Salt, to taste
Black pepper, to taste

Skewers, either metal or bamboo

Directions
1. Prepare the balsamic sauce at home by combining all the ingredients in a jar.
2. Place lid on and shake to combine well.
3. **If using bamboo skewers, let them soak 30 minutes in water before using.**
4. At the campsite, heat the grill to medium to high heat.
5. Thread the skewers into the vegetables.
6. Shake the balsamic sauce in the jar well before brushing generously on the prepared skewers.
7. Put the skewers on the grill and cook for about 5–8 minutes on each side or until the vegetables are softened and brown around the edges.
8. Remove the veggie skewers from the grill and serve.

Nutrition per serving
Calories 363, fat 19 g, carbs 44 g, sugar 15 g,
Protein 10 g, sodium 43 mg

Skewered Potatoes

Most people love potatoes; this recipe is made by cooking baby potatoes over the grill with spices and oil.

Serves 4 | Prep. time 10 minutes | Cooking time 10 minutes

Ingredients
24 baby potatoes
1 tablespoon vegetable oil
Salt and black pepper to taste
Garlic powder to taste

Skewers, either metal or bamboo

Directions
1. If using bamboo skewers, let them soak 30 minutes in water before using.
2. Preheat the grill or campfire to low-medium heat.
3. In a large bowl, add all the ingredients; toss to combine well.
4. Thread the skewers into the potatoes.
5. Place the skewers on the grill and cook for about 10–15 minutes or until cooked through.
6. Remove the skewers from the grill and serve.

Nutrition per serving
Calories 435, fat 20 g, carbs 60 g, sugar 3 g,
Protein 6 g, sodium 725 mg

DESSERTS

Strawberry Shortcake Skewers

These shortcake skewers need no cooking and are made by threading pound cake and strawberries on the skewers, and then covered in whipped cream! A quick and easy dessert perfect for rainy days.

Serves 4 | Prep. time 10 minutes

Ingredients
1 small store-bought pound cake, cut into ½-inch-thick slices and quartered
Whipped cream in a can as needed
4 large strawberries, sliced

4 skewers, either metal or bamboo

Directions
1. Put 1 piece of pound cake on a plate, cover with one slice of strawberry, and repeat the layers 3 more times. Finish off with a piece of the pound cake.
2. Thread one skewer carefully into the cake tower. Cover the skewers with whipped cream on one side.
3. Repeat and make 3 more skewers and serve.

Nutrition per serving
Calories 543, fat 49 g, carbs 24 g, sugar 17 g,
Protein 3 g, sodium 116 mg

Fruit Skewers

Fruits are rich in nutrition and delicious to eat. These skewers are made with different fruits. These are rainbow in color.

Serves 4 | Prep. time 5 minutes

Ingredients
2 medium bananas, sliced
2 medium kiwis, sliced
2 medium oranges, peeled
8 medium strawberries, sliced
8 green grapes

Directions
1. Thread the fruit into the skewer in your desired order and serve.

Nutrition per serving
Calories 121, fat 1 g, carbs 30 g, sugar 20 g,
Protein 2 g, sodium 3 mg

Campfire Chocolate Biscuit Cups

Kids and adults alike will love these biscuit cups filled with ready-made chocolate pudding and topped with whipped cream and almonds. These cups are quick and easy to make with only a few ingredients.

Makes 8 | Prep. time 5 minutes | Cooking time 15 minutes

Ingredients
1 package refrigerated small biscuit dough
12 ounces chocolate pudding ready to eat
2 tablespoons slivered almonds, crushed
Whipped topping in a can

Tarts on fire campfire sticks or woof'em or cobbler sticks

Directions
1. Divide the biscuit dough into 8 equal parts.
2. Stretch and flatten each biscuit dough to a flat circle in your hand.
3. Stretch one biscuit dough over one cobbler stick, and smooth out the creases. Make sure the dough is ¼-inch thick for even and quick cooking.
4. Place the biscuit dough sticks over the campfire and cook for about 5–10 minutes or until evenly browned; rotate frequently. For helpful tips on making campfire biscuit cups, go to page 4.
5. Remove the biscuit sticks from the campfire and let them cool for about 5–10 minutes before carefully removing the biscuit cups from the sticks.
6. Fill each biscuit cup evenly with pudding.
7. To serve, top generously with whipped topping and sprinkle with almonds.

Nutrition per serving
Calories 274, fat 12 g, carbs 38 g, sugar 12 g,
Protein 4 g, sodium 415 mg

Marshmallow Strawberry Toast Sticks

These sticks are made by threading the marshmallow and strawberry on the skewer and toasting them over the grill.

Serves 6 | Prep. time 5 minutes | Cooking time 5 minutes

Ingredients
18 marshmallows, large
12 strawberries, large
Chocolate sauce for serving

6 skewers, either metal or bamboo

Directions
1. If using bamboo skewers, let them soak 30 minutes in water before using.
2. Thread the marshmallow, then strawberry, again marshmallow, again strawberry, and again marshmallow onto a skewer; repeat and prepare 6 skewers in the same order.
3. Preheat the grill to low heat.
4. Place the prepared skewers on the grill and cook for about 3–5 minutes or until the marshmallows start to brown.
5. Serve with chocolate sauce.

Nutrition per serving
Calories 82, fat 0.11 g, carbs 20 g, sugar 13 g,
Protein 0.24 g, sodium 20 mg

French Custard Biscuit Cups

Another family favorite that you can make with biscuit cups. Make more, they'll disappear quickly!

Makes 4 | Prep. time 5 minutes | Cooking time 10 minutes

Ingredients
½ package refrigerated small biscuit dough
¾ cup prepared vanilla custard or vanilla pudding
¼ cup chocolate chips
Whipped cream topping in a can
Fresh berries for serving

Tarts on fire campfire sticks or woof'em or cobbler sticks

Directions
1. Divide the biscuit dough into 4 equal parts.
2. Stretch and flatten each biscuit dough part to a circle in your hand.
3. Stretch one biscuit dough over a tart on a firestick, and smooth out the creases. Make sure the dough is ¼ inches thick for even and quick cooking.
4. Place the biscuit dough sticks over the campfire and cook for about 5–10 minutes or until evenly browned; rotate frequently. For helpful tips on making campfire biscuit cups, go to page 4.
5. Remove the biscuit sticks from the campfire and let them cool for about 5–10 minutes before carefully removing the biscuit cups from the sticks.
6. Fill each biscuit cup evenly with custard cream.
7. Sprinkle the chocolate chips over the custard on each cup, top with whipped topping. Decorate with fresh berries if desired and serve.

Nutrition per serving
Calories 214, fat 9 g, carbs 30 g, sugar 8 g,
Protein 5 g, sodium 370 mg

Blueberry Campfire Biscuit Cups

These biscuit cups are tempting and super easy to make by cooking the biscuit dough over the campfire and filling it with blueberry pie filling, whipped cream, and fresh blueberries.

Makes 8 | Prep. time 5 minutes | Cooking time 5 minutes

Ingredients
1 package refrigerated small biscuit dough
11-ounce can blueberry pie filling
Whipped cream in a can (or other favorite whipped topping)
Fresh blueberries for serving

Tarts on fire campfire sticks or woof'em or cobbler sticks

Directions
1. Cut the dough into 8 equal parts.
2. Wrap and mold 1 part of the biscuit dough around the outside of a tart on a fire stick; repeat to prepare each.
3. Place the biscuit dough sticks over the campfire and cook for about 5–10 minutes or until evenly browned; rotate frequently. For helpful tips on making campfire biscuit cups, go to page 4.
4. Remove the biscuit sticks from the campfire and let them cool for about 5–10 minutes before carefully removing the biscuit cups from the sticks.
5. Fill each biscuit cup evenly with the blueberry pie filling, top with whipped cream and fresh blueberries, and serve.

Nutrition per serving
Calories 518, fat 52 g, carbs 49 g, sugar 22 g,
Protein 6 g, sodium 399 mg

Peach Cobbler Campfire Biscuit Cups

Makes 8 | Prep. time 10 minutes | Cooking time 15 minutes

Ingredients
Filling
1 cup canned peaches in juice, drained or 2 ripe fresh peaches, cored, peeled, and diced
⅔ cup brown sugar
¼ cup butter
2 teaspoons flour
1 tablespoon Bourbon whiskey, optional

Other ingredients
1 package refrigerated small biscuit dough
Whipped cream or whipped topping in a can

Directions
1. To make the filling, in a skillet over medium heat, melt butter. Add flour and stir for about 1-2 minutes.
2. Add sugar and stir until mixed well into the butter.
3. Add peaches and Bourbon, if using.
4. Let it simmer until the sauce thickens, stirring occasionally.
5. Remove from heat and let cool while the biscuit cups are cooking.
6. Divide the biscuit dough into 8 equal parts.
7. Stretch and flatten each biscuit dough to a flat circle in your hand.
8. Stretch one biscuit dough over one cobbler stick, and smooth out the creases. Make sure the dough is ¼-inch thick for even and quick cooking.
9. Place the biscuit dough sticks over the campfire and cook for about 5–10 minutes or until evenly browned; rotate frequently. For helpful tips on making campfire biscuit cups, go to page 4.
10. Remove the biscuit sticks from the campfire and let them cool for about 5–10 minutes before carefully removing the biscuit cups from the sticks.
11. Spoon the filling evenly into the biscuit cups.

12. Top with whipped cream, if desired, and serve.

Nutrition per serving
Calories 294, fat 12 g, carbs 44 g, sugar 21 g,
Protein 3 g, sodium 619 mg

S'mores Biscuit Cups

Another way to make S'mores that is not messy and so delicious. It will make all campers young and old very grateful!

Makes 8 | Prep. time 15 minutes | Cooking time 10 minutes

Ingredients
1 package refrigerated small biscuit dough
8 marshmallows, quartered or ¾ cup mini marshmallows or as needed
8 graham crackers, crushed
Chocolate sauce as needed
Whipped cream in a can, optional

Directions
1. Divide the biscuit dough into 8 equal parts.
2. Stretch and flatten each biscuit dough to a flat circle in your hand.
3. Stretch one biscuit dough over one cobbler stick, and smooth out the creases. Make sure the dough is ¼-inch thick for even and quick cooking.
4. Place the biscuit dough sticks over the campfire and cook for about 5–10 minutes or until evenly browned; rotate frequently. For helpful tips on making campfire biscuit cups, go to page 4.
5. Remove the biscuit sticks from the campfire and let them cool for about 5–10 minutes before carefully removing the biscuit cups from the sticks.
6. Layer the bottom of each cup with marshmallows, crushed crackers, and chocolate sauce in a biscuit cup. Top with whipped cream if desired, and serve.

Nutrition per serving
Calories 407, fat 13 g, carbs 67 g, sugar 30 g,
Protein 4 g, sodium 665 mg

Watermelon Pizza

These are refreshing watermelon pizza sticks made that are grilled and decorated with candies. The kids will love this.

Serves 6 | Prep. time 10 minutes | Cooking time 6 minutes

Ingredients
1 thick watermelon slice (about ¾-inch thick) cut into 6 wedges with the rind on
Salt to taste
M&M chocolates or other similar chocolates
Pecans or other favorite nuts

6 wooden popsicle sticks soaked in water 30 minutes before using

Directions
1. Prepare the grill for medium heat.
2. Insert a stick in each watermelon wedge in the middle of the rind.
3. Sprinkle a pinch of salt on the watermelon wedges.
4. Grill the watermelon wedges on each side for 2-3 minutes per side. Remove from heat.
5. Let each camper decorate their watermelon pizza by pushing into the watermelon's flesh the candies and nuts.

Nutrition per serving
Calories 195, fat 18 g, carbs 23 g, sugar 19 g, Protein 2 g, sodium 282 mg

RECIPE INDEX

BREAKFAST   **13**
   Cree Bannock Bread   13
   Stick Bread   14
   Croissant Fruit and Cheese Sticks   15
   Cinnamon Roll-Ups   16
   Bacon on a Stick   17
   Egg in an Orange   18
   Breakfast Campfire Biscuits Cup   19

APPETIZERS AND SIDES   **21**
   Wrapped Brussels Sprouts   21
   Cherry Feta Olive Salad Sticks   22
   Skewered Mushrooms   23
   Crispy Accordion Potatoes   24
   Zucchini and Smoked Salmon Rolls   25
   Caprese Salad Skewers   26
   Easy Shrimp Skewers   27
   Cuban Sandwich Sticks   28
   Sesame Tuna Bites   29
   Brat Skewers   30

CHICKEN   **31**
   Smoked Rotisserie Chicken   31
   Peruvian Chicken Skewer   33
   BBQ Chicken Skewers   35
   Mexican Chicken Skewers   37
   Piri Piri Chicken Sticks   38
   Salsa Chicken Sticks   39
   Campfire Biscuit Cups with BBQ Chicken   41

BEEF, PORK, AND LAMB   **43**
   Steak on a Stick   43
   Beef Kabobs   45
   Hot Dog Wrapped in Dough   46
   Cumin Lamb Skewers   47
   Grilled Teriyaki Pork   48
   Filipino BBQ Pork   49
   Morocco Kofta Balls   51

Grilled Hawaiian Steak Skewers	52
Grilled Pork Chops	53
Pizza Campfire Biscuit Cups	55
Sausage Skewers	56
SEAFOOD	**57**
Fish on a Stick	57
Grilled Garlic Shrimp	58
Teriyaki Tuna Skewers	59
Tuna Kebabs with Herbs, Lemon, and Grains	60
Campfire Biscuit Cups with Shrimp Salad Filling	61
VEGETARIAN	**63**
Cheesy Eggplant Skewers	63
Corn With Butter and Herbs	64
Zucchini and Cherry Skewers	65
Ratatouille Kebabs	66
Rainbow Veggie Skewers	67
Skewered Potatoes	69
DESSERTS	**71**
Fruit Skewers	71
Strawberry Shortcake Skewers	71
Campfire Chocolate Biscuit Cups	73
Marshmallow Strawberry Toast Sticks	74
French Custard Biscuit Cups	75
Blueberry Campfire Biscuit Cups	76
Peach Cobbler Campfire Biscuit Cups	77
S'mores Biscuit Cups	79
Watermelon Pizza	80

APPENDIX

Cooking Conversion Charts

1. Measuring Equivalent Chart

Type	Imperial	Imperial	Metric
Weight	1 dry ounce		28g
	1 pound	16 dry ounces	0.45 kg
Volume	1 teaspoon		5 ml
	1 dessert spoon	2 teaspoons	10 ml
	1 tablespoon	3 teaspoons	15 ml
	1 Australian tablespoon	4 teaspoons	20 ml
	1 fluid ounce	2 tablespoons	30 ml
	1 cup	16 tablespoons	240 ml
	1 cup	8 fluid ounces	240 ml
	1 pint	2 cups	470 ml
	1 quart	2 pints	0.95 l
	1 gallon	4 quarts	3.8 l
Length	1 inch		2.54 cm

Numbers are rounded to the closest equivalent

2. Oven Temperature Equivalent Chart

Fahrenheit (°F)	Celsius (°C)	Gas Mark
220	100	
225	110	¼
250	120	½
275	140	1
300	150	2
325	160	3
350	180	4
375	190	5
400	200	6
425	220	7
450	230	8
475	250	9
500	260	

* Celsius (°C) = T (°F)-32] * 5/9
** Fahrenheit (°F) = T (°C) * 9/5 + 32
*** Numbers are rounded to the closest equivalent

Printed in Great Britain
by Amazon